International Security Programs Benchmark Report

International Security Programs Benchmark Report
Research Report

Bob Hayes
Kathleen Kotwica

ELSEVIER

AMSTERDAM • BOSTON • HEIDELBERG • LONDON
NEW YORK • OXFORD • PARIS • SAN DIEGO
SAN FRANCISCO • SINGAPORE • SYDNEY • TOKYO

Security
Executive Council

Elsevier
The Boulevard, Langford Lane, Kidlington, Oxford, OX5 1GB, UK
25 Wyman Street, Waltham, MA 02451, USA

First published 2013

Notices
Knowledge and best practice in this field are constantly changing. As new research and experience broaden our understanding, changes in research methods, professional practices, or medical treatment may become necessary.

Practitioners and researchers must always rely on their own experience and knowledge in evaluating and using any information, methods, compounds, or experiments described herein. In using such information or methods they should be mindful of their own safety and the safety of others, including parties for whom they have a professional responsibility.

To the fullest extent of the law, neither the Publisher nor the authors, contributors, or editors, assume any liability for any injury and/or damage to persons or property as a matter of products liability, negligence or otherwise, or from any use or operation of any methods, products, instructions, or ideas contained in the material herein.

British Library Cataloguing in Publication Data
A catalogue record for this book is available from the British Library

Library of Congress Cataloging-in-Publication Data
A catalog record for this book is available from the Library of Congress

ISBN: 978-0-12-411593-4

For more publications in the Elsevier Risk Management and Security Collection, visit our website at **store.elsevier.com/SecurityExecutiveCouncil**

This book has been manufactured using Print On Demand technology. Each copy is produced to order and is limited to black ink. The online version of this book will show color figures where appropriate.

Working together
to grow libraries in
developing countries

www.elsevier.com • www.bookaid.org

Printed and bound by CPI Group (UK) Ltd, Croydon, CR0 4YY

Transferred to digital print 2013

CONTENTS

EXECUTIVE SUMMARY

In the *International Security Programs Benchmark Report*, the findings of a broad research survey conducted by the Security Executive Council are presented and analyzed. The data suggests that international security programs are greatly affected by company size and the location of the security department within the organization, whether as part of the executive, legal, or human resources function. This report identifies the types of security baseline programs that are in place for international security programs and describes the organizational perception of security's role and capability. This report provides security leaders with valuable insights into the scope of international security programs at key corporations with contextualized comparison points for evaluating their own programs.

WHAT IS A RESEARCH REPORT?

A research report provides the foundational information security practitioners need in order to review, understand, and successfully address key issues within the workplace. It presents current data collected and analyzed as a result of Security Executive Council research. The data comes from a range from small- and medium-sized businesses to some of the largest international corporations, across both the public and private sectors. This research report can be used by security professionals and managers who want to identify successful practices of their peers in the field to prepare a business case, develop a strategy, or incorporate findings for their security programs and services that mitigate risk. Educators can use this report for assignments, class projects, and scenario development and analysis.

Summary of Results

SURVEY BACKGROUND

Starting as a member strategic initiative, the Security Executive Council interviewed 12 member companies regarding the reach and breadth of their international security programs as compared to their domestic programs. What was identified from those interviews was a need for a larger survey, in which researchers sought to define the scope of current programs and to create a benchmark for what companies have in place. Experts analyzed the survey data collected over a 3-month period from 149 qualified respondents.

PROGRAM SIZE AND SCOPE

The majority of respondents came from large companies, with 60% from companies with revenues over $5 billion. More than half (60%) reported there are more than 1,000 employees in the organization, and the most often cited title was director of security (42%). Eighty percent of respondents had security responsibility for the entire organization, and the average number of direct reports (exempt) was 10.

The functional location of the security department proved to be a significant area of variance as far as responsibility for international security risk mitigation and program formal accountability. The top three functional areas the security department resided in were executive (23%), legal (20%), and human resources (11%).

When comparing level of responsibility for international security risk mitigation to where the security group functionally resides (the most reported functions), for example, the table below demonstrates the broad differences that emerged:

Level of Responsibility for International Security Risk Mitigation as Compared to Where the Security Group Functionally Resides			
	Executive (Where 23% of Security Groups Reside)	Legal (Where 20% of Security Groups Reside)	Human Resources (Where 11% of Security Groups Reside)
Security is responsible for policy/guidance/controls but has no operational responsibilities	31%	13%	41%
Security has responsibility for specific areas of risk similar to domestic operations that are aligned to international business areas	40%	60%	29%

BUDGET

For those that gave a clear response, time was the most often cited indicator (more than double the next cited indicator) to describe allocation type devoted to domestic and international programs; time was followed by resource allocation, department activities, and budget, respectively. The average frequency of allocation (regardless of indicator type) between domestic and international programs was 62% domestic and 38% international. However, there were a handful of respondents that made comments around the fact that they operated as a global company and didn't make distinctions between domestic and international programs. The business activities most often performed outside of the "home country" (home country is used to denote the country in which the parent corporation resides) were:

- Services—owned or managed by the organization (70%)
- Sales and marketing (66%)
- Partners, affiliates, or wholly owned subsidiaries (57%)
- Supply chain—owned or managed by the organization (47%)

RISK OVERSIGHT

Forty-four percent of security departments have responsibility for specific areas of risk that are similar to their domestic operations and that are aligned to international business areas.

Most had some form of risk oversight group but at varying levels of responsibility:

- A group that met on a regular basis: 27%
- A group that met in response to situations: 24%
- An *ad hoc* group or a group only in selected locations: 21%

Interestingly, when comparing Fortune 500 (F500) companies and Fortune 50,000 (F50K) companies,[1] 86% of F500 companies have risk oversight groups that meet on a regular basis, whereas only 15% of F50K companies have groups that meet regularly.

PERCEPTION OF INTERNATIONAL SECURITY PROGRAMS AND COMPLIANCE

When looking at all categories of respondents, only *some* international security programs or services are known within the organization, but not all are well known (42%). When comparing F500 to F50K companies, however, there was a broader disparity in perception. In 73% of F500 companies, *some* international security programs or services are known within the organization, but not all are well known; in F50K companies, that percentage dropped to only 27%.

A majority of companies (67%) have some kind of formal processes or procedures for discovery/tracking regulatory requirements per country. More than half (54%) have an established liaison between security and the legal department to remain current concerning country regulations and compliance measures.

TYPES OF SECURITY BASELINE PROGRAMS

There are various levels of security baseline programs in place for international security programs, ranging from those with formal objectives and budgets to those that only service as requested or needed. Governance of these programs also varied somewhat, though the top three choices that clearly emerged were corporate policy (59%), corporate guidelines (47%), and regulations and laws (35%).

---

[1]The Security Executive Council coined the "Fortune 50,000" term after recognizing that these companies had a need for security programs as well. Most prior studies focused primarily on Fortune 500 companies. "Fortune 50,000" refers to corporations with annual gross revenues above $50 million but below $5 billion.

In total, researchers asked about 25 different security baseline programs. In the table below, some highlights of the data about these programs are outlined. (The full data set is available in the following section.)

Existing Security Baseline Programs for International Security Programs: Selected Highlights					
Program	Not Applicable (%)	Planned, but Not Yet Implemented (%)	Formal Program Accountability (%)	Formal Program, Shared Responsibility (%)	Services as Requested (%)
Awareness and Education	7	17	34	20	22
Brand, reputation, trademark/trade name	17	9	24	26	26
Business continuity/ resiliency	11	15	30	33	12
Business ethics and compliance	11	5	29	41	14
Emergency response and disaster recovery	6	13	30	40	11
Incident reporting	3	11	44	30	13
Information security systems and specifications	15	10	32	34	9
Information security intellectual property protection	14	11	26	36	13
Product protection (e.g., tampering, counterfeiting, diversion)	31	7	15	23	24
R&D security	39	8	21	14	18
Risk assessments	5	5	40	27	23
Security-related regulations and compliance management	7	8	36	32	17
Supply chain security	28	10	19	26	17
Travel security	8	9	43	23	17

When further breaking down the data in the above table, it becomes apparent that there are variances along lines of functional location (executive, legal, or human resources branches) and company size (F500 or F50K). For example, when comparing the functional location of security in those companies that do have formal accountability for a brand, reputation, trademark/trade name program, 17% reside in the executive function, 14% in legal, and 9% in human resources. Looking at business continuity/resiliency formal program accountability, 16% reside in the executive function, 30% in legal, and 5% in human resources. Differences like these suggest that international security programs are affected by the functional location of security within the organization.

If company size is taken into account, the disparities are even greater: For companies that indicated formal program accountability of information security intellectual property protection, 63% belong to the F500 category as opposed to 37% for F50K companies. The trend continued when looking at brand, reputation, trademark/trade name programs—64% of companies with formal program accountability were F500 companies, whereas 36% were F50K. These differences appear to confirm that companies in the F500 category have more developed baseline security programs in their international security programs than their counterparts in the F50K.

Survey Data

DEMOGRAPHICS AND ORGANIZATIONAL STRUCTURE

Below is a summary of the data collected about the individuals included in the survey and their organizational structures.

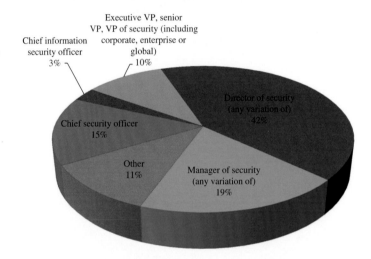

Titles of individuals participating in the survey.

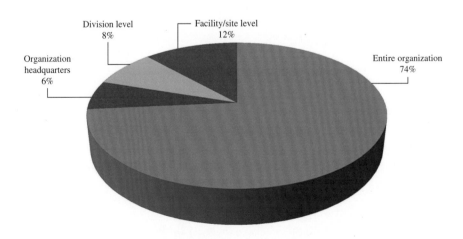

Scope of responsibility within the organization.

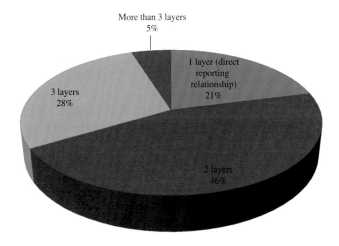

Layers of reporting from the home country company's senior-most operating executive (president or equivalent).

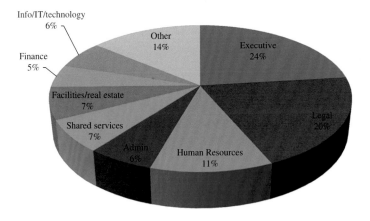

Where in the organization the security group functionally resides.

INDUSTRY

Below is a summary of the data collected about the organizations reflected in the survey. When asked about the industry each individual's organization belonged to, the highest level of Securities and Exchange Commission categorization was used for respondents to select from (also used by Hoover's business information service). *Note: there was not enough data to conduct industry-specific comparisons.*

The highest representation by industry was financial services (9%) followed by pharmaceuticals (6%). The next highest representation was tied between five industries at 5% each: healthcare, insurance, retail, security products and services, and telecommunications services.

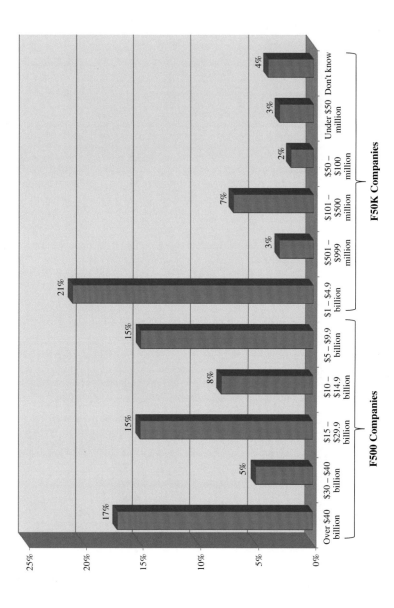

Annual gross sales or revenues (including all plants, divisions, branches, parents, and subsidiaries worldwide) of organizations reflected in the survey.

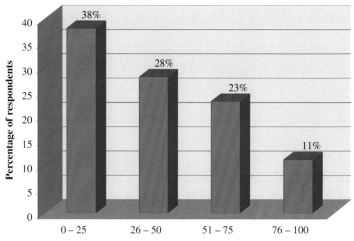

Percentage of corporate revenue that comes from sales of products, goods or services outside the home country market.

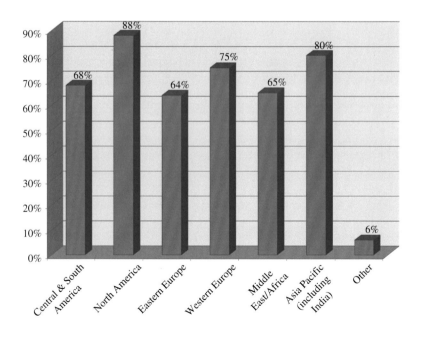

Regions companies operating in (respondents could choose multiple regions).

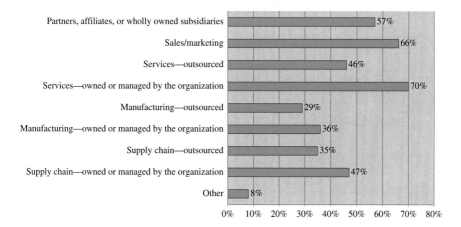

Business activities performed by the company outside of the home country (respondents could choose multiple activities).

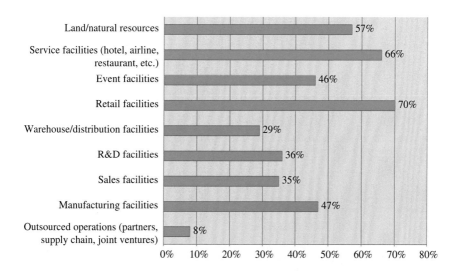

Types of physical facilities (leased or owned) corporations utilize outside of the home country (respondents could choose multiple types of facilities).

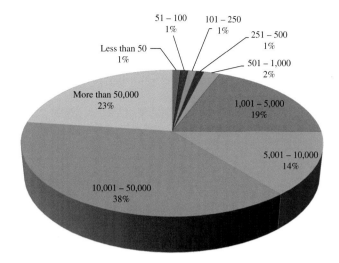

The number of employees worldwide for each respondent's organization.

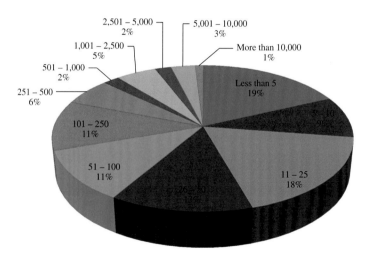

The number of security employees worldwide for each respondent's organization.

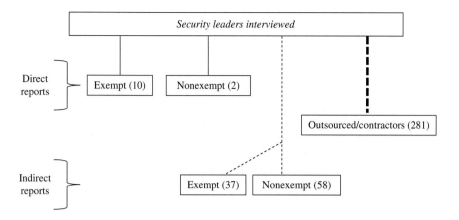

The average number of security employees among the security leaders interviewed.

Home Country of Each Respondent's Organization

Sixty-nine percent of respondents answered United States of America.

Percentage of overall budget, time, allocation of resources, or department activities, whichever was most meaningful to respondent, allocated to domestic compared to international security programs.

A. Meaningful indicator:

For those that gave a clear response, time was the most often cited indicator (more than double the next cited indicator), followed by resource allocation, department activities, and budget, respectively.

B. Percentages devoted to programs (added to 100%):

Domestic: 62%

International: 38%.

Note: The next two questions do not pertain to situations where organizations utilize nonemployees who are contractually bound to provide manufacturing or other services.

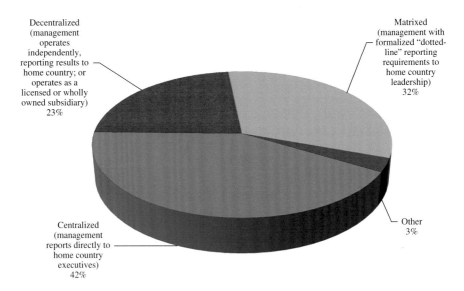

Decentralized (management operates independently, reporting results to home country; or operates as a licensed or wholly owned subsidiary) 23%

Matrixed (management with formalized "dotted-line" reporting requirements to home country leadership) 32%

Other 3%

Centralized (management reports directly to home country executives) 42%

Type of organizational structure the enterprise uses.

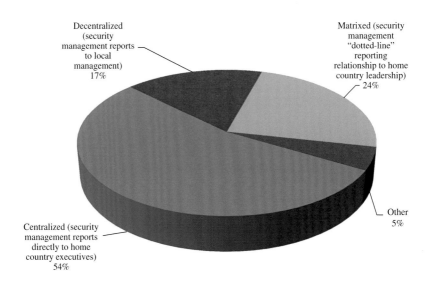

Decentralized (security management reports to local management) 17%

Matrixed (security management "dotted-line" reporting relationship to home country leadership) 24%

Other 5%

Centralized (security management reports directly to home country executives) 54%

Type of organizational structure the security department uses.

CORPORATE SECURITY INTERNATIONAL ORGANIZATIONAL ROLE

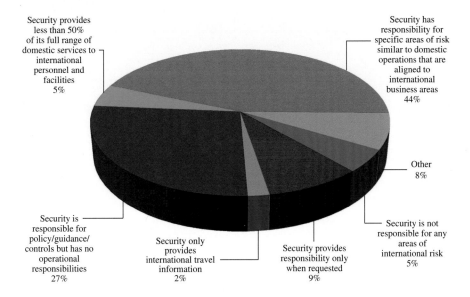

Security provides less than 50% of its full range of domestic services to international personnel and facilities
5%

Security has responsibility for specific areas of risk similar to domestic operations that are aligned to international business areas
44%

Other
8%

Security is responsible for policy/guidance/controls but has no operational responsibilities
27%

Security only provides international travel information
2%

Security provides responsibility only when requested
9%

Security is not responsible for any areas of international risk
5%

Security's overall level of responsibility for international security risk mitigation.

	Reports to Executive (%)	Reports to Legal (%)	Reports to Human Resources (%)
Security is responsible for policy/guidance/controls but has no operational responsibilities	31	13	41
Security has responsibility for specific areas of risk similar to domestic operations that are aligned to international business areas	40	60	29

The table above compares the overall level of responsibility for international security risk mitigation to where security group functionally resides (most reported functions).

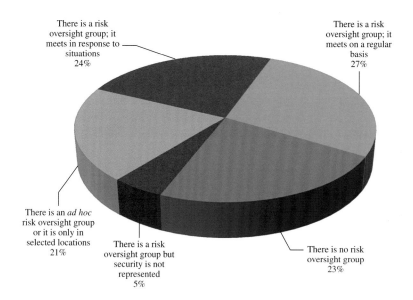

There is a risk oversight group; it meets in response to situations 24%

There is a risk oversight group; it meets on a regular basis 27%

There is an *ad hoc* risk oversight group or it is only in selected locations 21%

There is a risk oversight group but security is not represented 5%

There is no risk oversight group 23%

Corporate risk oversight team/group for international operations that includes security representation.

	F500 (%)	F50K (%)
There is a risk oversight group; it meets in response to situations	57	43
There is a risk oversight group; it meets on a regular basis	85	15

Respondents were asked whether their organizations had a risk oversight group, and if so, whether it meets in response to situations or on a regular basis. The table above breaks down those individuals that answered yes for either question by company size: F500 or F50K. For example, of all the respondents that indicated there is a risk oversight group that meets in response to situations, 57% of those were F500 companies, and 43% were F50K companies.

ORGANIZATIONAL PERCEPTION OF SECURITY'S ROLE AND CAPABILITY

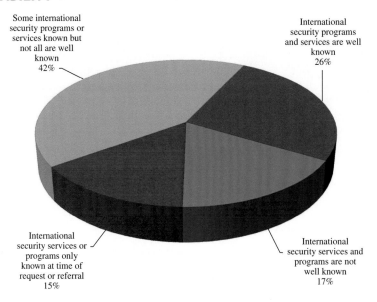

A breakdown of employee awareness of international security programs within the enterprise.

	F500 (%)	F50K (%)
International security services and programs are not well known	43	57
International security services or programs only known at time of request or referral	43	57
Some international security programs or services known but not all are well known	73	27
International security programs and services are well known	69	31

Respondents were asked to assess how well international security services or programs are known within their organizations. Each of the four results in the table above was then broken down by company size: F500 or F50K. For example, of all the respondents that indicated international security services and programs are *not* well known, 43% of those were F500 companies, and 57% were F50K companies.

Overall capabilities and services of the security personnel in the international program as compared to the domestic program (1 = poor, 10 = exceptional).

Domestic: 8.0

International: 6.2

Overall nonsecurity personnel's awareness of security staff's international security competence and expertise (1 = poor, 10 = exceptional).

Nonsecurity personnel awareness: 5.1

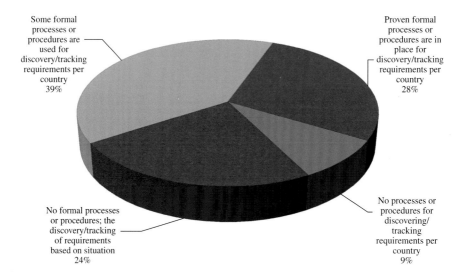

Some formal processes or procedures are used for discovery/tracking requirements per country
39%

Proven formal processes or procedures are in place for discovery/tracking requirements per country
28%

No formal processes or procedures; the discovery/tracking of requirements based on situation
24%

No processes or procedures for discovering/ tracking requirements per country
9%

Type of processes or procedures in place for discovering/tracking regulatory requirements per country.

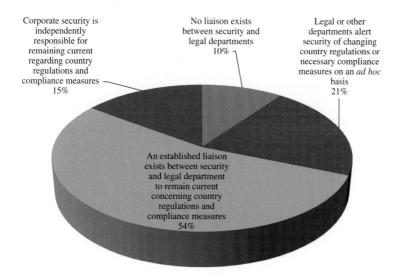

Corporate security is independently responsible for remaining current regarding country regulations and compliance measures
15%

No liaison exists between security and legal departments
10%

Legal or other departments alert security of changing country regulations or necessary compliance measures on an *ad hoc* basis
21%

An established liaison exists between security and legal department to remain current concerning country regulations and compliance measures
54%

Level of cooperation established between corporate security and the legal business group to develop information and security programs to comply with country regulations.

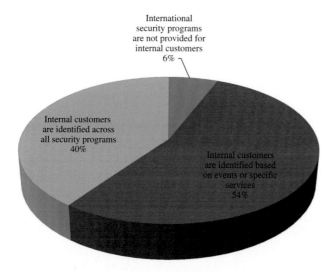

International security programs are not provided for internal customers
6%

Internal customers are identified across all security programs
40%

Internal customers are identified based on events or specific services
54%

How security identifies internal business customers for services provided by security's international security programs.

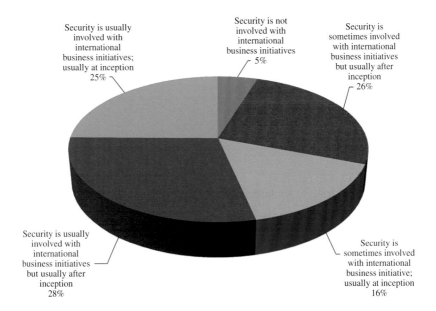

When and how often security becomes involved with an international business initiative.

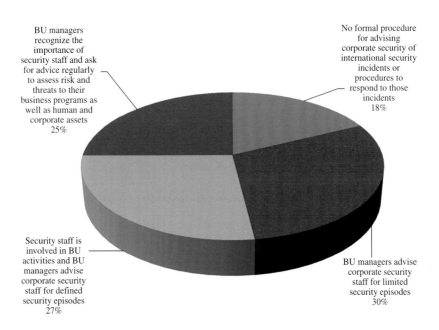

Level of communication coming in from nonhome country business units (BUs) regarding international security issues.

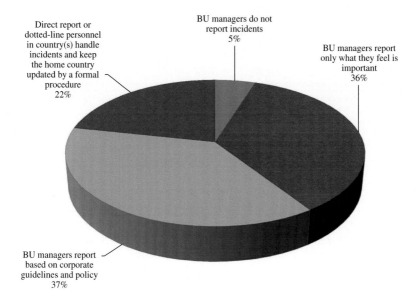

Direct report or
dotted-line personnel
in country(s) handle
incidents and keep
the home country
updated by a formal
procedure
22%

BU managers do not
report incidents
5%

BU managers report
only what they feel is
important
36%

BU managers report
based on corporate
guidelines and policy
37%

Procedures in place for reporting international security-related incidents.

PROGRAMS

The table below represents the 25 security baseline programs with formal objectives and budget or services as requested or needed that are in place for the international security program.

Existing Security Baseline Programs for International Security Programs

Program	Not Applicable (%)	Planned, but Not Yet Implemented (%)	Formal Program Accountability (%)	Formal Program, Shared Responsibility (%)	Services as Requested (%)
Asset protection, loss prevention	14	9	23	31	23
Aviation security and operations	47	5	19	13	17
Awareness and education	7	17	34	20	22
Brand, reputation, trademark/trade name	17	9	24	26	26
Business continuity/resiliency	11	15	30	33	12
Business ethics and compliance	11	5	29	41	14
Business intelligence and analysis	19	9	28	17	26
Emergency response and disaster recovery	6	13	30	40	11
Incident reporting	3	11	44	30	13
Information security systems and specifications	15	10	32	34	9
Information security intellectual property protection	14	11	26	36	13
Investigations (e.g., theft, fraud, threats, due diligence, conflict of interest)	5	7	42	28	18
IT forensic investigation	22	7	28	22	21
Law enforcement liaison	5	7	48	16	25
New product and marketing security	30	8	18	17	26
Personnel protection/workplace violence	8	9	40	24	18

Personnel screening, background investigations, and due diligence	12	7	29	36	16
Physical site security design and system specifications	7	4	44	30	16
Product protection (e.g., tampering, counterfeiting, diversion)	31	7	15	23	24
R&D security	39	8	21	14	18
Risk assessments	5	5	40	27	23
Security-related regulations and compliance management	7	8	36	32	17
Security/business command center	24	15	33	13	15
Supply chain security	28	10	19	26	17
Travel security	8	9	43	23	17

The four charts below break down the respondents who indicated that their organizations do have formal program accountability for specific programs by the function in which security resides.

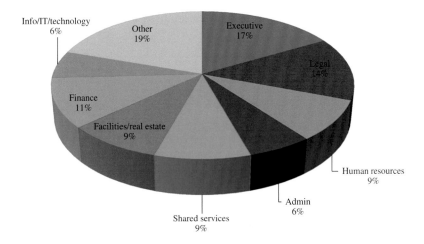

Location of security within the organization for companies that do have a formal brand, reputation, trademark/ trade name program.

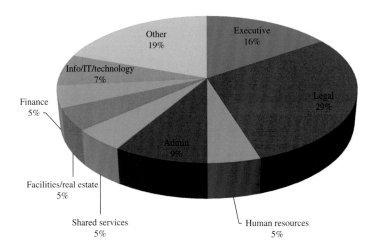

Location of security within the organization for companies that do have a formal business continuity/resiliency program.

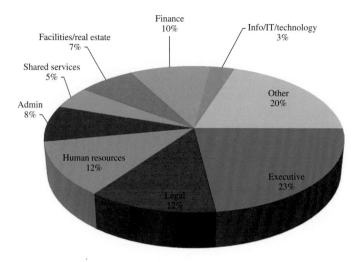

Location of security within the organization for companies that do have a formal program for risk assessments.

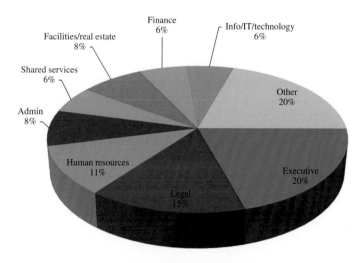

Location of security within the organization for companies that do have a formal program for security-related regulations and compliance management.

Comparing formal program accountability of information security, intellectual property protection between F500 and F50K companies.

F500: 63%

F50K: 37%

Comparing formal program accountability of brand, reputation, trademark/trade name between F500 and F50K companies.

F500: 64%

F50K: 36%

STANDARDS, POLICIES, AND PROCEDURES

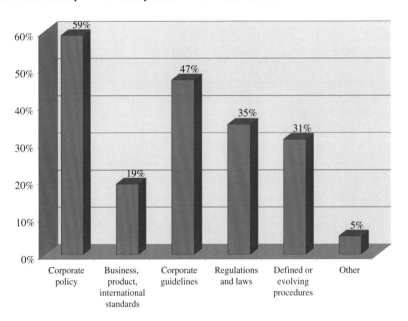

The methods by which the international security program is governed (respondents were limited to a maximum of three choices).

OTHER

The following were identified as key areas needing further research by interviewees:

- Travel security, return on investment, and relevant tools and services
- International security issues, such as the use of consultants, best practices for legal and regulatory compliance in multiple countries, and adapting security training to local situations
- Asset protection, measuring retail shrinkage internationally

- IP protection, particularly in an international context
- Company interaction with US Government, State Department, and Defense Security Service
- Diversity, leadership, and strategy creation
- Vendors and security control

Bob Hayes has more than 25 years of experience developing security programs and providing security services for corporations, including 8 years as the CSO at Georgia Pacific and 9 years as security operations manager at 3M. His security experience spans the manufacturing, distribution, research and development, and consumer products industries as well as national critical infrastructure organizations. Additionally, he has more than 10 years of successful law enforcement and training experience in Florida and Michigan. Bob is a recognized innovator in the security field and was named as one of the 25 Most Influential People in the Security Industry by *Security Magazine*. He is a frequent speaker at key industry events. He is a leading expert on security issues and has been quoted by such major media outlets as the *Wall Street Journal* and *Forbes*. Bob is currently the managing director of the Security Executive Council.

Kathleen Kotwica has a PhD in experimental psychology from DePaul University and has had a career as a researcher and knowledge strategist. Her experience includes positions as information architecture consultant at a New England consulting firm, director of online research at CXO Media (IDG), and research associate at Children's Hospital in Boston. She has authored and edited security industry trade and business articles and has spoken at security-related conferences including CSO Perspectives, SecureWorld Expo, ASIS, and CSCMP. In her current role as EVP and chief knowledge strategist at the Security Executive Council, she leads the development and production of Council tools, solutions, and publications. She additionally conducts industry research and analysis to improve security and risk management practices.

About Elsevier's Security Executive Council Risk Management Portfolio

Elsevier's Security Executive Council Risk Management Portfolio is the voice of the security leader. It equips executives, practitioners, and educators with proven information and practical solutions for successful security and risk management programs. This portfolio covers topics in the areas of risk mitigation and assessment, ideation and implementation, and professional development, and brings trusted risk management advice, tactics, and tools to business professionals. Previously available only to Security Executive Council members, this research-based content—covering corporate security, enterprise crisis management, global IT security, and more—provides real-world solutions and "how-to" applications to implement new physical and digital risk management strategies and build successful security and risk management programs.

Elsevier's Security Executive Council Risk Management Portfolio is a key part of the *Elsevier Risk Management and Security Collection.* The collection provides a complete portfolio of titles for the business executive, practitioner, and educator by bringing together the best imprints in risk management, security leadership, digital forensics, IT security, physical security, homeland security, and emergency management: Syngress, which provides cutting-edge computer and information security material; Butterworth Heinemann, the premier security, risk management, homeland security, and disaster-preparedness publisher; and Anderson Publishing, a leader in criminal justice publishing for more than 40 years. These imprints, along with the addition of Security Executive Council content, bring the work of highly regarded authors into one prestigious, complete collection.

The Security Executive Council (www.securityexecutivecouncil.com) is a leading problem-solving research and services organization focused on helping businesses build value while improving their ability to effectively manage and mitigate risk. Drawing on the collective knowledge of a large community of successful security practitioners, experts, and strategic alliance partners, the Council develops strategy and insight and identifies proven practices that cannot be found anywhere else. Our research, services, and tools are focused on protecting people, brand, information, physical assets, and the bottom line.

Elsevier (www.elsevier.com) is an international multimedia publishing company that provides world-class information and innovative solutions tools.

ALSO AVAILABLE IN ELSEVIER'S SECURITY EXECUTIVE COUNCIL RISK MANAGEMENT PORTFOLIO

Nine Practices of the Successful Security Leader
Research Report
March 2013

Establishing the Value of All-Hazards Risk Mitigation
Proven Practices
March 2013

General Security Guidelines
Template
Forthcoming, June 2013

Bringing a Corporate Security Culture to Life
Proven Practices
Forthcoming, September 2013

Printed and bound by CPI Group (UK) Ltd, Croydon, CR0 4YY

08/05/2025

01864941-0001